Love Songs for Ukulele

by Dick Sheridan

37 SONGS IN ALL
A WIDE RANGE OF SELECTIONS
FOR PLAYERS OF ALL AGES

ISBN 978-1-57424-290-4
SAN 683-8022

Cover by James Creative Group

Copyright © 2013 CENTERSTREAM Publishing, LLC
P.O. Box 17878 - Anaheim Hills, CA 92817

www.centerstream-usa.com

DEDICATION

To my parents …
For the first ukulele
under the Christmas tree.
For the baritone uke,
a high school graduation gift
that went to college.
For a musical household
whose memories are ever present.

Love Songs
for
Ukulele

ABOUT THE AUTHOR

Although a bachelor and never married, Dick claims to have the soul of a true romantic. As such he feels qualified to present these songs of love and passion, many of which have been with him since childhood. The ukulele also goes back to Dick's early years. It was a Christmas gift whose mystery and magic have remained with him ever since. Other instruments have come along, and Dick learned to play each in turn, the guitar, the mandolin, and the 5-string and tenor banjos. For over 40 years he has led a Dixieland Jazz Band with which he plays tenor banjo. What started as an avocational pursuit while teaching in the public schools, Dick has also privately taught all of the fretted string instruments, and his students number in the hundreds. Truly a sentimentalist and despite his advancing maturity, Dick avows that he is not a bachelor by choice and is ready and willing to serenade with his ukulele any fair maiden kindly disposed to give him a wink and the "come hither."

~oOo~

4

INTRODUCTION

It's true, love makes the world go 'round. In every country of the world throughout the ages from time immemorial, love has been celebrated. And not just in music alone but in all the arts – painting, poetry, dance, literature. Now enter the ukulele …

Whether the music is classical, folk, from Tin Pan Alley, or one of the chart-topping popular tunes of the day, the uke can play it all. One of the humblest of all musical instruments, the diminutive uke nonetheless has a significant voice which easily captures the full range of emotions that you'll find in the wide variety of love songs that follow.

Apart from its sweet and mellow sound, what is the attraction of the ukulele? First of all, it is small and portable. A basic instrument can be purchased at a reasonable price. It is relatively easy to play, and no barrage of amplification equipment is needed. By itself or with other instruments, for melodies or chord harmonies, it is an ideal instrument for a host of musical occasions, not the least of which are ones of love and romance.

Love songs! Poignant, festive, happy, sad, whimsical – their range seems unlimited. Songs of courtship and affection, fulfillment and hopeful expectation, even tragic songs of broken hearts and rejection – they're all at your fingertips.

From fondly recalled love songs of yesteryear to those that are just as popular today as when they were first written, there's plenty of fun and enjoyment in store for you and your uke in the following pages.

Let the music begin and the good times roll! The Love Bug's gonna get you!

THE ABA DABA HONEYMOON

Ukulele tuning: gCEA

ARTHUR FIELDS

WALTER DONOVAN

THE ABA DABA HONEYMOON

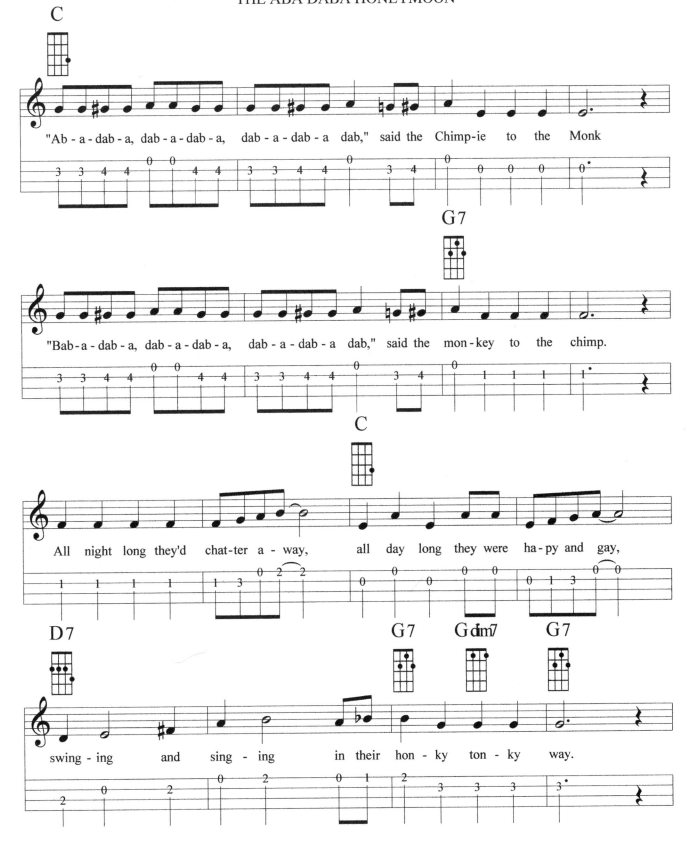

THE ABA DABA HONEYMOON

ABA DABA HONEYMOON: The term "anthropomorphic" (describing human characteristics to non-human objects) certainly applies to this song of monkey love. There are numerous other examples, "Froggie Went A-Courting" being just one of them. Debbie Reynolds and Carleton Carpenter sang the song in the 1950 movie *Two Weeks With Love*. Their duet hit the charts the following year as did several other versions of the song including one by songwriter Hoagy Carmichael ("Stardust" and "Georgia On My Mind").

SHINE ON, HARVEST MOON

Ukulele tuning: gCEA

JACK NORWORTH

SHINE ON HARVEST MOON: As with many popular songs, the title of this song became the title of a movie. Ann Sheridan and Jack Carson starred in the 1944 film depicting the life of composer Jack Norworth and his wife, Nora Bayes, who was a vaudeville teammate. Norworth also collaborated with Albert Von Tilzer for "Take Me Out To The Ball Game."

AVALON

Ukulele tuning: gCEA

AL JOLSON
B. G. DeSILVA

VINCENT ROSE

I found my love in Av - a - lon _____ be -

side _____ the bay, _____ I left my love in

Av - a - lon, _____ and sail'd _____ a - way. _____ I

dream of her and Av - a - lon _____ from dusk _____ till

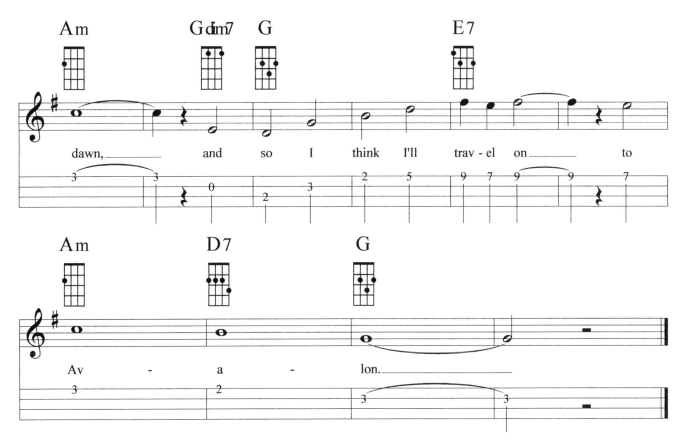

AVALON: Together with Vincent Rose and Buddy DeSylva, Al Jolson is listed as co-composer, although his name might well have been added only to entice sales, a popular ploy of publishers at the time. Rose, a bandleader and prolific songwriter ("Whispering," "Linger Awhile," and "Blueberry Hill) probably wrote the music and DeSylva the lyrics. DeSylva was one of Tin Pan Alley's top songwriters who later went on to co-found Capitol Records. A successful lawsuit was filed against "Avalon" claiming it lifted the melody from Puccini's opera *Tosca*. There was an award of $25,000 and the loss of all future royalties from print music sales. However a royalty of $1.00 was permitted for performances, and that amount eventually far exceeded the court award. The song remains a popular jazz standard.

BEAUTIFUL DREAMER

Ukulele tuning: gCEA

STEPHEN C. FOSTER

BEAUTIFUL DREAMER

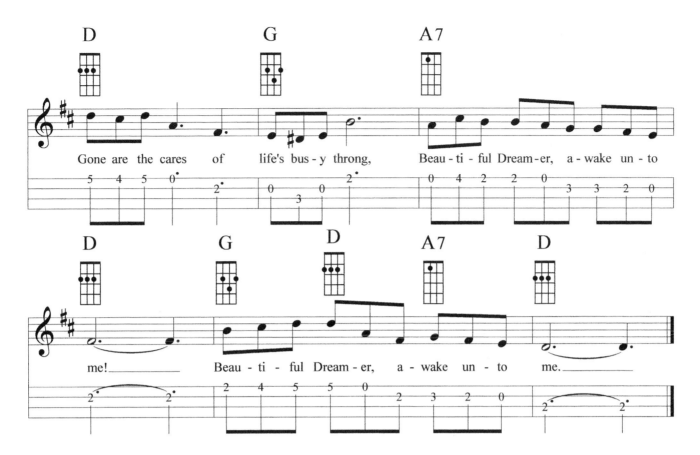

Gone are the cares of life's bus-y throng, Beau-ti-ful Dream-er, a-wake un-to me! Beau-ti-ful Dream-er, a-wake un-to me.

2. Beautiful Dreamer, out on the sea,
   Mermaids are chanting their wild Lorelei.
   Over the streamlet vapors are borne,
   Waiting to fade at the bright coming morn.
   Beautiful Dreamer, beam on my heart,
   E'en as the moon on the streamlet and sea;
   Then will all clouds of sorrow depart,
   Beautiful Dreamer, awake unto me!
   Beautiful Dreamer, awake unto me!

Stephen Foster's output was prodigious, and no American music is more treasured. From the bouncy "Oh! Susanna" to the romantic "Beautiful Dreamer" and "Jeanie With The Light Brown Hair," his songs capture a range of moods and emotions, some gentle with sentimental words and melodies, some high-spirited and jubilant. Although many of Foster's lyrics were written with an Afro-American dialect, they are not offensive and were penned with an affection and compassionate ear for the speech of the time. How tragically sad that his life should have ended in poverty and alcoholism, separated from wife and children, robbed of royalties and recognition, selling tunes for the price of a drink. From early minstrel days, through vaudeville, and on into the repertoires of classical divas, parlor performers, folk singers, and bluegrass bands, his songs have stood the test of time and are truly immortal.

BEAUTIFUL DREAMER: Published in 1864, just months after Stephen Foster's death, it is considered by some to be the last song that Foster wrote. There is evidence to the contrary, however, that a first edition was copyrighted two years earlier. Whatever, it is one of Foster's last songs and certainly one of his most cherished. The 9/8 rhythm requires nine strums per measure divided into three groups of three strums each.

CARELESS LOVE

Ukulele tuning: gCEA

Traditional

CARELESS LOVE

2. Love my mama and my papa too,
   Love my mama and my papa too,
   Love my mama and my papa too,
   But I'd leave them both to go with you.

3. When my apron strings were low, (3 times)
   You'd hardly ever pass my door.

4. But now my apron strings won't pin, (3 times)
   You pass my door and won't come in.

5. Cried last night and the night before, (3)
   I'll cry tonight and then no more.

6. Sorrow, sorrow, in my heart, (3)
   Since my love and I did part.

CARELESS LOVE: Folk music abounds with songs of unrequited love, broken hearts, and jilted lovers. The opposing emotions of love and hate often come to the fore in ballads that go back for centuries, and that certainly is true for the heart-wrenching themes of many operas and country western ditties.

CUDDLE UP A LITTLE CLOSER

Ukulele tuning: gCEA

OTTO HARBACH

KARL HOSCHNA

CUDDLE UP A LITTLE CLOSER: There'd be no resistance to a ukulele player armed with this song and "Put Your Arms Around Me, Honey." Defenses would crumble, caution thrown to the winds. The author and publisher of this book assume no responsibility.

DAISY BELL
(A Bicycle Built For Two)

Ukulele tuning: gCEA

HARRY DACRE

DAISY BELL: Better know perhaps as "A Bicycle Built For Two," this favorite waltz harks back to the days of gaslights and the horse & buggy. Have you ever tried riding a two-seater bicycle? It's not as easy as it looks!

FOR ME AND MY GAL

Ukulele tuning: gCEA

EDGAR LESLIE &
E. RAY GOETZ

GEORGE W. MEYER

FOR ME AND MY GAL: Here's one of those songs whose title was used for a movie, this one a 1942 production with Judy Garland and Gene Kelly. Ray Goetz and Edgar Leslie wrote the lyrics and publisher George Meyer the music as he did for "If You Were The Only Girl In The World" and a trad jazz band number called "Mandy, Make Up Your Mind." Among Leslie's other songs are "Moon Over Miami," "When Ragtime Rosie Ragged The Rosary," and "It Looks Like Rain In Cherry Blossom Lane." Both Leslie and Goetz were charter members of ASCAP (American Society of Composers, Authors and Publishers). Goetz's sister Dorothy was married to Irving Berlin but died of typhoid fever only six months after the wedding.

FRANKIE AND JOHNNY

Ukulele tuning: gCEA

Traditional

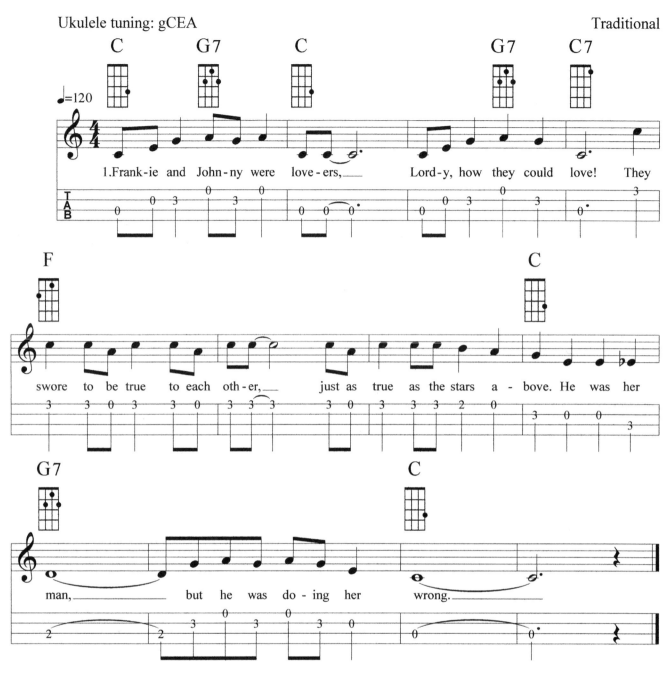

2. Frankie and Johnny went walking,
   Johnny in his brand new suit,
   "Oh, good Lord!" says Frankie,
   "Don't my Johnny look real cute."
   He was her man, but he was doin' her wrong.

3. Johnny says, "I've got to leave you,
   But I won't be gone very long.
   Don't wait up for me, Frankie,
   Or worry while I'm gone."
   He was her man, but he was doin' her wrong.

3. Frankie went down to the pool hall,
   To buy herself a bottle of beer,
   She says to the fat bartender,
   "Has my Johnny-man been here?"
   He was her man, but he was doin' her wrong.

4. The bartender looks at Frankie,
   Looks her right in the eye,
   "Ain't gonna tell you no story,
   Ain't gonna tell you no lie,
   If he's your man, he's a-doin' you wrong."

5. "Ain't gonna tell you no story,
   Ain't gonna tell you no lie,
   I saw your Johnny 'bout an hour ago
   With a gal named Nellie Bly.
   If he's your man, he's a-doin' you wrong."

6. Frankie goes down to South 12th Street,
   Looks up in the window so high,
   And there she sees her Johnny
   A-kissin' that Nellie Bly,
   He was her man, but he was doin' her wrong.

7. Frankie pulls back her kimono,
   Pulls out an old Forty-Four,
   Rooty-toot-toot, that gal did shoot,
   And Johnny rolled over the floor,
   He was her man, but he was doin' her wrong.

8. There six men goin' to the graveyard,
   Six in an old-time hack,
   Six men goin' to the graveyard,
   But only five are comin' back,
   He was her man, but he was doin' her wrong.

9. This story ain't got no moral,
   This story ain't got no end,
   This story just goes to show you
   That there ain't no good in men,
   They'll do you wrong, just as sure as your born.

FRANKIE AND JOHNNY: Like "Careless Love," here's another classic example of a love affair gone bad, a man "who done her wrong," and hell hathing no fury like a woman scorned.

GYPSY LOVE SONG

Ukulele tuning: gCEA

HARRY B. SMITH

VICTOR HERBERT

GYPSY LOVE SONG: On a personal note, this was one of my dad's favorites. It was a signature song from the Victor Herbert operetta *The Fortune Teller* of 1898. The lyricist, Harry Smith, also wrote the words to "The Sheik Of Araby," which was written in response to the success of Rudolph Valentino's iconic film *The Sheik*. "The Sheik Of Araby" has become a standard for trad jazz bands and was being played in New York City by clarinetist and jazz buff Woody Allen the night he received word of winning the Oscar for his film *Annie Hall*.

I GAVE MY LOVE A CHERRY

Ukulele tuning: gCEA

Traditional Folk Song

2. How can there be a cherry without a stone,
   How can there be a chicken that has no bone,
   How can there be a ring that has no end,
   How can there be a baby with no cryin'?

3. A cherry when it's blooming, it has no stone,
   A chicken when it's pipping, it has no bone,
   A ring when it's rolling, it has no end,
   A baby when it's sleeping, there's no cryin'.

I GAVE MY LOVE A CHERRY: Riddle songs have long been popular in folk music. Some promise a reward if the questions are answered correctly. Here are some conundrums found in other songs: What is louder than a horn (thunder), sharper than a thorn (grief), deeper than a well (Torah), higher than a house (chimney), faster than a mouse (cat), etc. A suitor might quiz or be quizzed to determine acceptability as a wedding prospect.

I KNOW MY LOVE

Ukulele tuning: gCEA

Traditional Irish

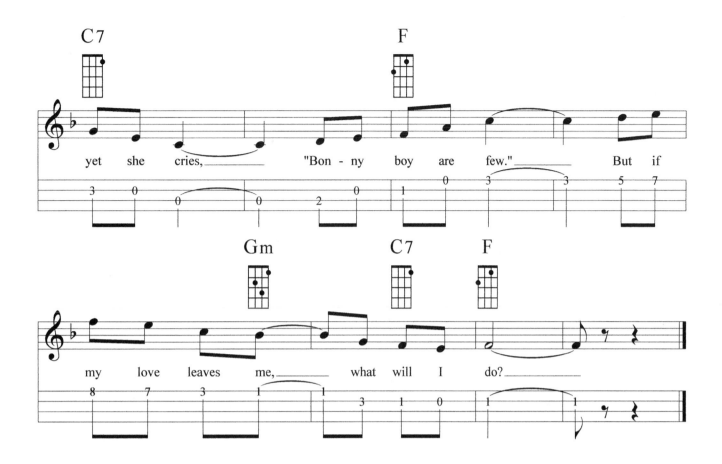

2. There is a dance hall in Maradyke,
And there my love goes every night
And sits upon some strange lad's knee,
Well, don't you know now, that vexes me.
And yet she cries, "I love him the best."
But a troubled mind, sure, can know no rest.
And yet she cries, "Bonny boys are few."
But if my love leaves me, what will I do?

I KNOW MY LOVE: I feel sorry for the singer of this folk song that comes from Ireland. The lad is obviously enamored of his lady love, but despite her avowal of mutual affection, she likes to play the field. The singer's sense of uncertainty and frustration is palpable. Time to move on, me bucko.

I NEVER WILL MARRY

Ukulele tuning: gCEA

Traditional Folk Song

I NEVER WILL MARRY

Both the verses and the chorus of this song share the same melody.

1. One day as I rambled
   Down by the seashore,
   The wind it did whistle,
   And the waves they did roar.

2. I heard a fair maiden
   Give a pitiful cry,
   And it sounded so lonely
   As it swept off on high.

3. CHORUS

4. "The shells in the ocean
   Will be my death bed,
   The waves of dark water
   Will wash o'er my head."

5. She cast her fair body
   In the water so deep,
   She closed her pretty blue eyes
   Forever to sleep.

I NEVER WILL MARRY: Marriage is not for everyone. The unmarried way of life for many bachelors and bachelorettes is by choice. But such appears not to be so in this sadly beautiful old ballad. Was it rejection, unfaithfulness, love of another, disinterest? We'll never know the answer. It lies beneath the waves with the song's poor heroine. A variant of this song is called "Little Mohee." It tells of a sailor who rejects the love of an Indian chieftain's daughter. Returning home to an unfaithful sweetheart, he realizes his folly and sets sail back across the ocean to his Indian maiden.

I LOVE YOU TRULY

Ukulele tuning: gCEA

CARRIE JACOBS-BOND

I love you tru - ly, tru - ly, dear.

Life with its sor - row, life with its tear,

fades in - to dreams when I feel you are near,

for I love you tru - ly, tru - ly, dear.

I LOVE YOU TRULY: Very few weddings of yesteryear were without this song being rendered from the chapel choir loft or other celebration venue. Times have changed and more contemporary songs have come along, but few rival the lovely sentiments and melody of this enduring classic.

I WANT A GIRL

Ukulele tuning: gCEA

I WANT A GIRL: The Von Tilzer brothers – Harry, Julie, Jack, Will and Albert – created a family dynasty of music publishers and songwriters. Harry, who wrote this song's music with lyrics by Will Dillon, was one of Tin Pan Alley's most successful songwriters. Harry's brother Albert wrote such memorable songs as "Oh By Jingo!" and "Put Your Arms Around Me, Honey" (both included in this collection). Perhaps Albert's best known song is "Take Me Out To The Ballgame" ironically written years before he ever saw his first baseball game.

I WONDER WHO'S KISSING HER NOW

Ukulele tuning: gCEA

WILL M. HOUGH
& FRANK R. ADAMS

JOSEPH E. HOWARD
& HAROLD ORLOB

I WONDER WHO'S KISSING HER NOW

I WONDER WHO'S KISSING HER NOW: Although Joe E. Howard was listed as composer on sheet music that sold millions of copies, it was later discovered that an arranger hired by Howard – Harold Orlob – was the real writer. Orlob kept this quiet until a biographical movie of Howard's life came out with the same title as the song. Following a heated court battle, Orlob gained credit as co-writer but sacrificed any financial gain unlike Howard who had profited enormously.

I'M FALLING IN LOVE WITH SOMONE

Ukulele tuning: gCEA

RITA JOHNSON YOUNG

VICTOR HERBERT

I'M FALLING IN LOVE WITH SOMEONE

I'M FALLING IN LOVE WITH SOMEONE: Together with "Ah! Sweet Mystery Of Life" and "Italian Street Song" these songs from the operetta *Naughty Marietta* are among Victor Herbert's most successful. Before opening on Broadway in 1910, the show was premiered a few months earlier in my nearby city of Syracuse, New York. The libretto was one of many for Rida Johnson Young who also wrote the lyrics for "Mother Machree," much favored by Irish tenors like the celebrated John McCormack.

IF YOU WERE THE ONLY GIRL IN THE WORLD

Ukulele tuning: gCEA

CLIFFORD GREY

NAT D. AYER

IF YOU WERE THE ONLY GIRL IN THE WORLD

IF YOU WERE THE ONLY GIRL IN THE WORLD: Nat Ayer, an American, collaborated on this song with the English writer Clifford Grey. Ayer also wrote "Oh! You Beautiful Doll" for the English theater, this time with lyricist Seymour Brown. Grey was something of a dark horse. While in America under an assumed name, he joined a bobsled team that won gold medals in the Winter Olympics of 1928 and 1932 and a bronze in 1937. He died in 1941 of a heart attack and other complications shortly after a bombing raid in Suffolk, England where he had been performing for British troops.

IN THE GOOD OLD SUMMERTIME

Ukulele tuning: gCEA

REN SHIELDS

GEORGE EVANS

IN THE GOOD OLD SUMMERTIME

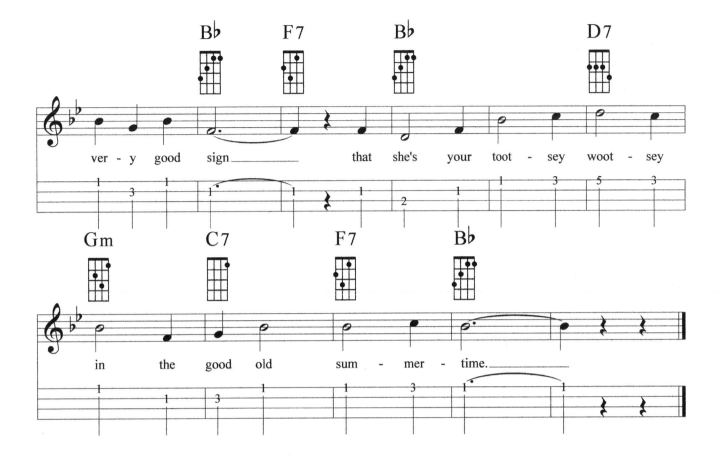

IN THE GOOD OLD SUMMERTIME: Up pops Judy Garland again (see "Under The Bamboo Tree'), this time with Van Johnson, in the 1949 film that shares the same title as that of the song. When the song was written in 1902, it was initially turned down by publishers who felt it too seasonal. But a friend of the writing team, Blanche Ring, introduced it in a show in which she was performing, *The Defenders*. The audience loved it and sang along with her on the chorus. The song gained popularity on the vaudeville circuit, and when it was eventually published sales skyrocketed, a million sheet music copies were sold, and the popularity continues to this day.

IDA

Ukulele tuning: gCEA

EDDIE LEONARD

EDDIE MUNSON

IDA

My band can never remember which tune is "Ida" and which is "Dinah."
Just to set the record straight, this tune is "Ida" and the other one *is not.*

IDA: Eddie Leonard who wrote the lyrics and first popularized the song was one of the last performers from the minstrel show era. Comedian Eddie Cantor, with his bulging "banjo eyes," did a vaudeville imitation of Leonard whose trademark was a white suit, white top hat, and slow drawl with stretched-out syllables. The song became one of Cantor's favorite numbers, not the least of reasons being that his wife's name was Ida.

THE LOVE NEST

Ukulele tuning: gCEA

LOUIS HIRSCH

THE LOVE NEST

LOVE NEST: Fans of the Burns & Allen comedy shows on both radio and TV will recognize this as their familiar theme song of marital bliss. Composer Lou Hirsch wrote the song for the musical comedy Mary produced in 1920. He was one of the co-founders of ASCAP in 1914, later a director from 1917 to 1924.

MA
(HE'S MAKING EYES AT ME)

Ukulele tuning: gCEA

SIDNEY CLARE

CON CONRAD

MA (HE'S MAKING EYES AT ME): Other songs by lyricist Sidney Clare include "Please Don't Talk About Me When I'm Gone" and the Dixieland standard "Big Butter And Egg Man." In the song list for composer Con Conrad we find "Margie," "Barney Google," "You've Got To See Your Mama Every Night," and the novelty number "Palesteena" popularized by Groucho Marx.

MARGIE

Ukulele tuning: gCEA

BENNY DAVIS

CON CONRAD &
J. RUSSEL ROBINSON

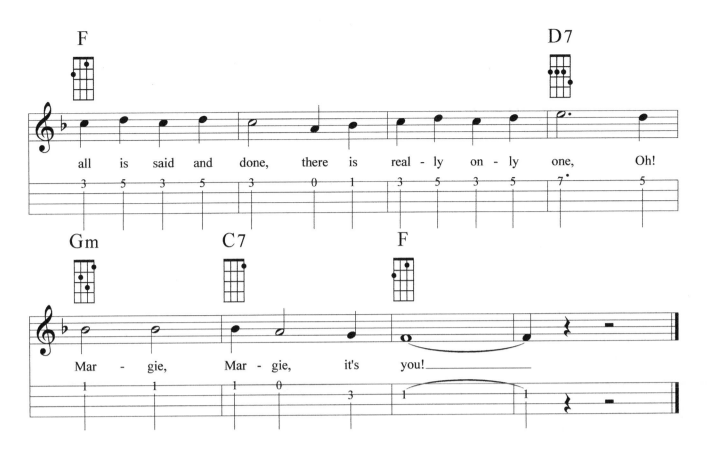

MARGIE: Introduced in December of 1920 on a Victor label recording by the Original Dixieland Jazz Band. Co-composer of the song was the band's pianist J. Russel Robinson. Eddie Cantor's young daughter was the inspiration for the song's title.

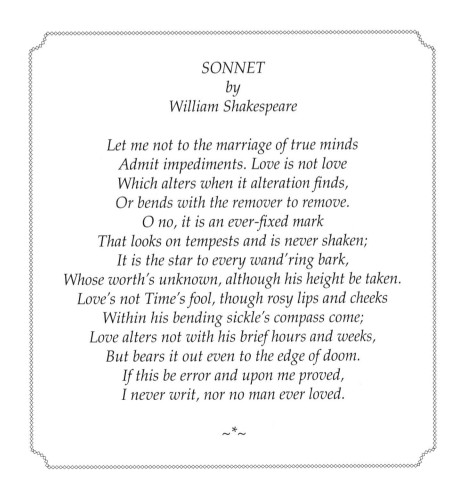

SONNET
by
William Shakespeare

Let me not to the marriage of true minds
Admit impediments. Love is not love
Which alters when it alteration finds,
Or bends with the remover to remove.
O no, it is an ever-fixed mark
That looks on tempests and is never shaken;
It is the star to every wand'ring bark,
Whose worth's unknown, although his height be taken.
Love's not Time's fool, though rosy lips and cheeks
Within his bending sickle's compass come;
Love alters not with his brief hours and weeks,
But bears it out even to the edge of doom.
If this be error and upon me proved,
I never writ, nor no man ever loved.

~*~

LOVE'S OLD SWEET SONG

Ukulele tuning: gCEA

G. CLIFTON BINGHAM   JAMES LYNAM MOLLOY

LOVE'S OLD SWEET SONG: How restful and peaceful is this gentle song with its quieting feeling of relaxation and repose. How vivid the imagery of "flick'ring shadows that softly come and go." It brings to mind a line from Longfellow's poem *The Children's Hour:* "Comes a pause in the day's occupations …"

MOONLIGHT BAY

Ukulele tuning: gCEA

EDWARD MADDEN

PERCY WENRICH

MOONLIGHT BAY: One of the many "moon" songs linked to love and romance. What would be a hayride, a beach party, an evening sail, or a crackling campfire without the nostalgia and sweet harmony this tune evokes?

MY GAL SAL

Ukulele tuning: gCEA

PAUL DRESSER

They called her friv-o-lous Sal,_____ a pe-cu-liar sort of a gal,_____ with a heart that was mel-low, an all-'round good fel-low, was my old pal._____ Your trou-bles, sor-rows and care_____ she was al-ways wil-ling to share;_____ a wild sort of dev-il, but

MY GAL SAL

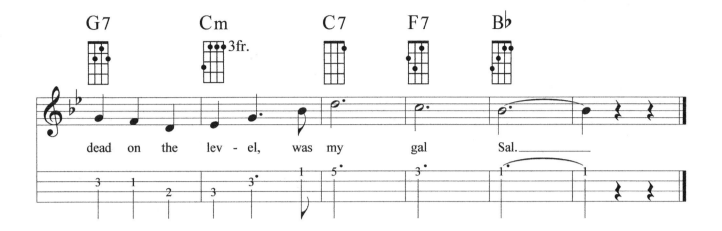

MY GAL SAL: Despite a difficult start in his early years – threat of reform school, prison time for petty thievery, and alienation from his father – composer Paul Dresser eventually found his niche on stage, singing and performing in a variety of acts. Success came when he began writing songs. His famous "On The Banks Of The Wabash" generated a fortune, and was one of the best selling sheet music songs of the 19th century. Dresser was a large man with large appetites. He weighed close to 300 pounds. Together with his brother, novelist Theodore Dresser, he squandered his money in the saloons and fleshpots of New York City. In today's dollars his fortune amounted to millions. But high living and generosity to family and friends ultimately led him to reduced circumstances. TV fans of the 50s and 60s may recall Jackie Gleason singing "My Gal Sal" at the opening and closing of his comedy sketch in which he portrayed "Joe, The Bartender." How sweet it was.

MY MELANCHOLY BABY

Ukulele tuning: gCEA

GEORGE A. NORTON

ERNIE BURNETT

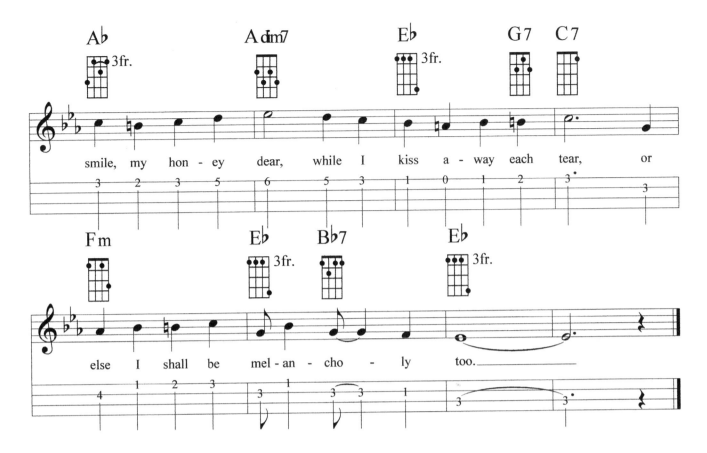

smile, my hon - ey dear, while I kiss a - way each tear, or

else I shall be mel - an - cho - ly too.

MY MELANCHOLY BABY: We all know the popular and vivid image: an inebriated patron, deep in his cups, wallowing in self-pity, staggers up to the house pianist, and with boozy, slurred speech makes the emphatic demand, "Play Melancholy Baby!"

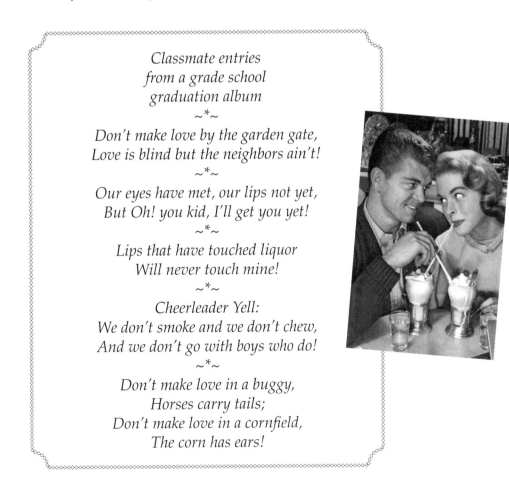

Classmate entries
from a grade school
graduation album
~*~

Don't make love by the garden gate,
Love is blind but the neighbors ain't!
~*~

Our eyes have met, our lips not yet,
But Oh! you kid, I'll get you yet!
~*~

Lips that have touched liquor
Will never touch mine!
~*~

Cheerleader Yell:
We don't smoke and we don't chew,
And we don't go with boys who do!
~*~

Don't make love in a buggy,
Horses carry tails;
Don't make love in a cornfield,
The corn has ears!

OH BY JINGO!

Ukulele tuning: gCEA

LEW BROWN   ALBERT VON TILZER

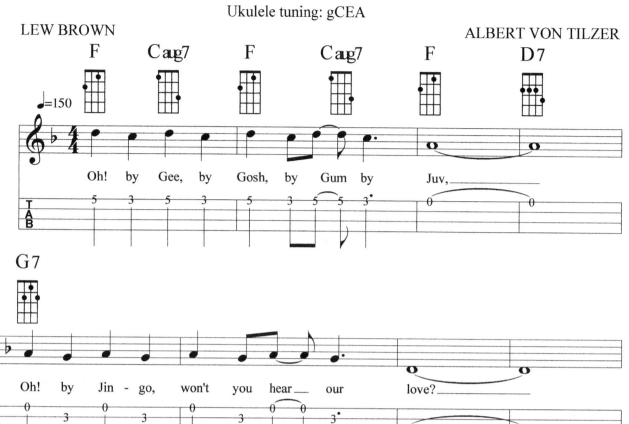

Oh! by Gee, by Gosh, by Gum by Juv,_____

Oh! by Jin - go, won't you hear ___ our love? _____

We will build for you a hut, you will be ___ our fav - 'rite nut,

we'll have a lot of lit - tle Oh! by Gol-lies, then we'll put them in the Fol - lies.

OH BY JINGO!: Here's a good companion song for "Aba Daba Honeymoon" and "We'll Build A Bungalow" also known as "The Zulu King" (both included in this collection). What fun these songs are with visions of swinging jungle vines, monkey chatter, and the beat of the village tom-toms.

OH! YOU BEAUTIFUL DOLL

Ukulele tuning: gCEA

SEYMOUR BROWN

NAT D. AYER

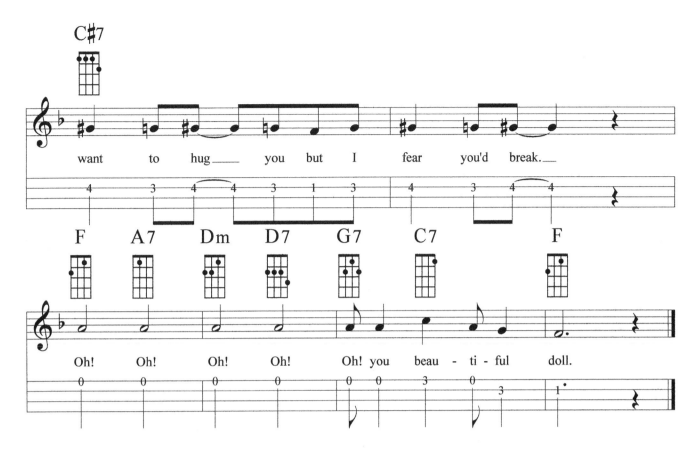

OH! YOU BEAUTIFUL DOLL: Many covers of sheet music at the turn of the Twentieth Century were works of art and are highly prized by collectors. The cover for this song may be an exception. A lovely deb is pictured with an oversized plumed hat the size of a giant space ship, an enormous Frisbee, or the gong cymbal from the opening of a *J. Arthur Rank* movie production. What limitation the cover art may have is more than compensated for by this upbeat song with its hint of ragtime inspiration.

PRETTY BABY

Ukulele tuning: gCEA

GUS KAHN

EGBERT VAN ALSTYNE

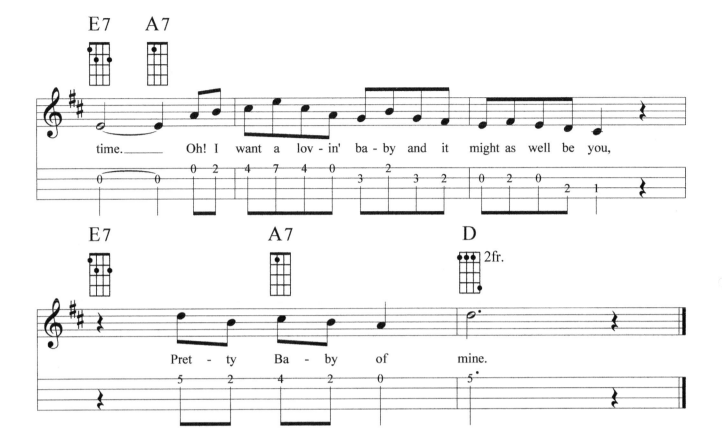

PRETTY BABY: Although the celebrated songwriting team of Kahn and Van Alstyne are usually credited with the song's composition, the published sheet music of 1916 also cites Tony Jackson, a popular New Orleans musician, who may in fact actually have been the song's creator.

PUT YOUR ARMS AROUND ME, HONEY

Ukulele tuning: gCEA

JUNIE McCREE

ALBERT VON TILZER

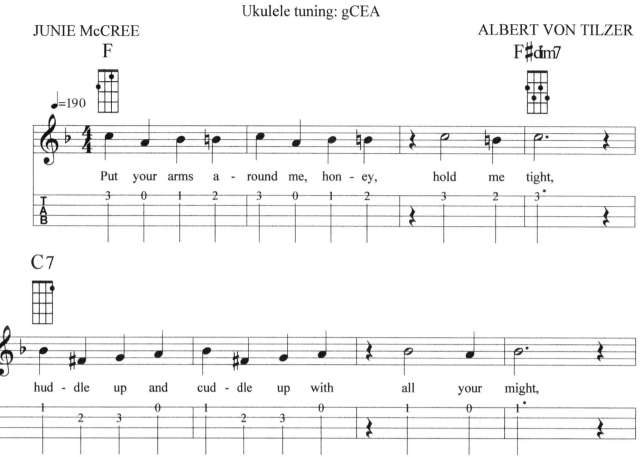

Put your arms a - round me, hon - ey, hold me tight,

hud - dle up and cud - dle up with all your might,

Oh! Oh! Won't you roll those eyes,

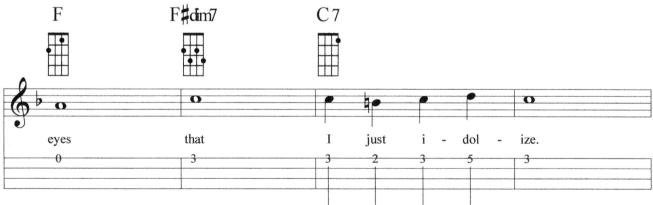

eyes that I just i - dol - ize.

PUT YOUR ARMS AROUND ME, HONEY

PUT YOUR ARMS AROUND ME, HONEY: This bouncy tune so perfectly captures the feeling of its lyrics. Can't you just feel the rocking motor boat and the exuberance and innocence of a good snuggle? And, of course, when all else fails, there's nothing like a hug and a squeeze to set the world right again.

SECRETS

Ukulele tuning: gCEA

F. J. KNOWLES

C. R. SMITH

then who can tell, she may whis - per, while the cit - y sleeps be - low, "I was

dream - ing of him when you woke me, but rose he must nev - er know."

SECRETS: Of all the glee club numbers we sang in college, this one lingers in memory far more than the rest. It is a touchingly sentimental love song that never fails to bring a tear on hearing it or reading the lyrics. The words are from a poem written by C. R. Smith and published at the turn of the 20th century. Its popularity gave rise to a number of musical interpretations, one version of which was by Mildred J. Hill. She and her sister Patty were the composers of the HAPPY BIRTHDAY song.

THE SHEIK OF ARABY

Ukulele tuning: gCEA

HARRY B. SMITH &
FRANCIS WHEELER

TED SNYDER

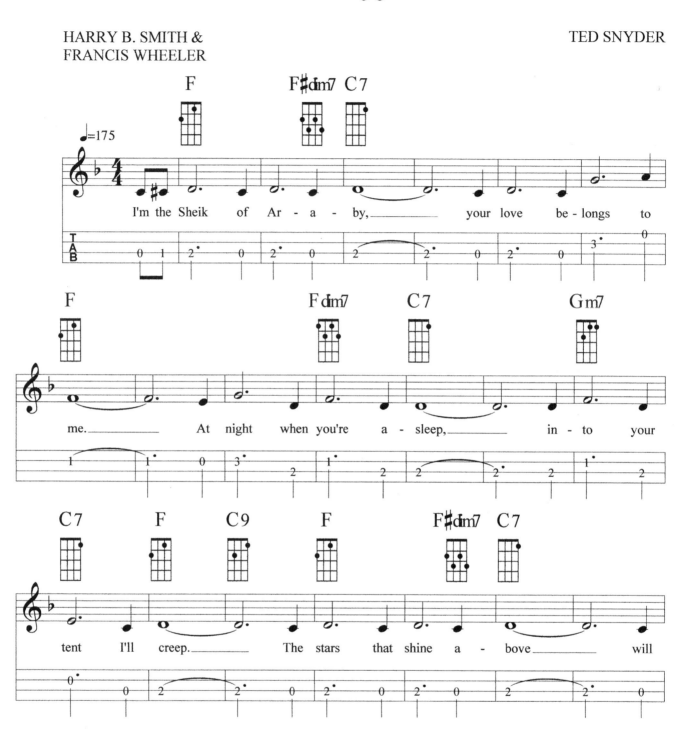

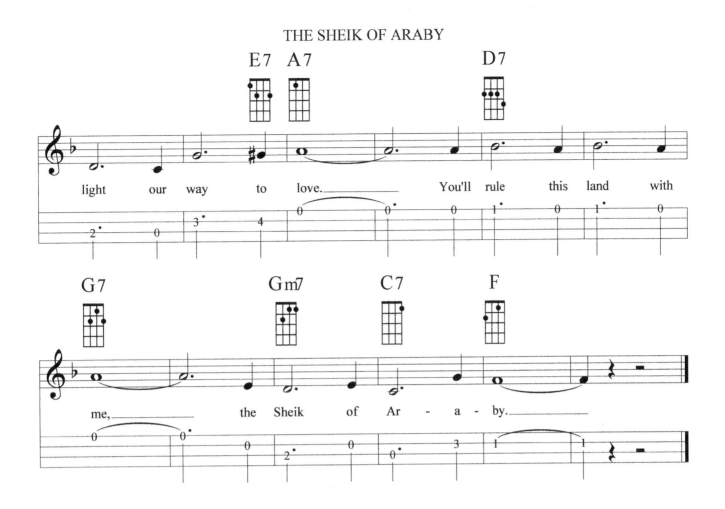

THE SHEIK OF ARABY: When the silent film *The Sheik* was released in 1921, it took the nation by storm. Rare was the maiden's heart that was not stirred by the film's leading man, Rudolph Valentino. Wasting no time, the song's composers jumped on the band wagon and published their work the same year. Although the film has been relegated to the archive vaults, the song lives on as a popular jazz standard. See the notes for "Gypsy Love Song."

UNDER THE BAMBOO TREE

Ukulele tuning: gCEA

BOB COLE

UNDER THE BAMBOO TREE: A memorable movie scene comes from the 1944 film *Meet Me In St. Louis*. At a family party Judy Garland and Margaret O'Brien (then about six or seven years old) perform this number doing a song & dance vaudeville routine, complete with straw hats and canes. It is truly fun -- one of Hollywood's most delightful musical moments!

WE'LL BUILD A BUNGALOW

Ukulele tuning: gCEA

Traditional

WE'LL BUILD A BUNGALOW

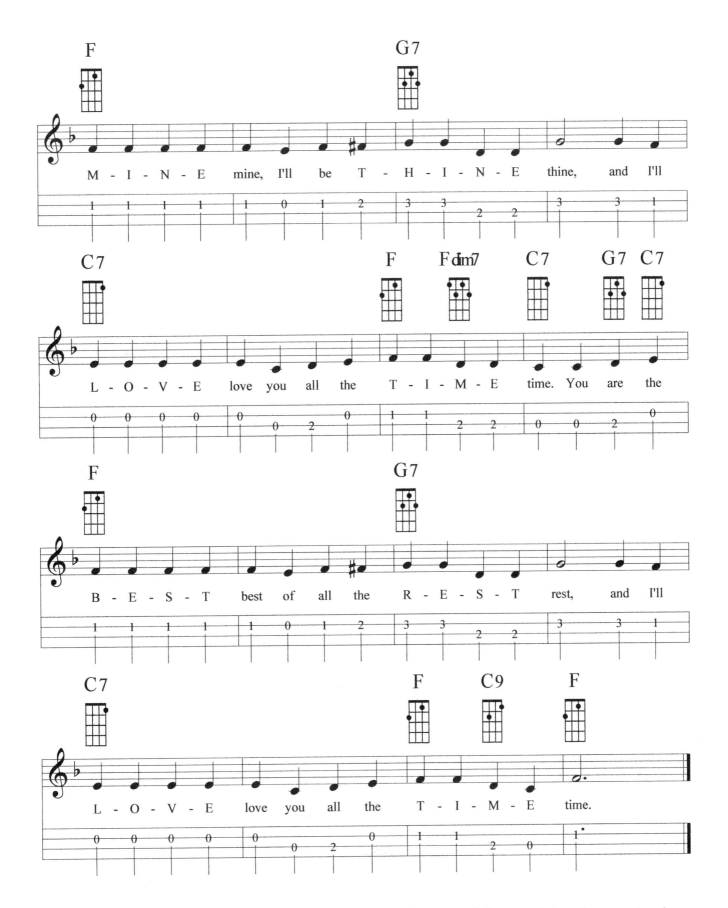

WE'LL BUILD A BUNGALOW: Here's a children's favorite that's stood the test of time for camping, bus trips, and family car rides that have helped parents sidestep the "Are we there yet?" syndrome. It's part of a larger song called "The Zulu King."

PAPER OF PINS

Ukulele tuning: gCEA

Traditional

(He) 2. I'll give to you a coach and six, with all the horses black as pitch, if you will marry me, etc.
(She)   I'll not accept your coach and six, with all the horses black as pitch, and I'll not marry you, etc.

(He) 3. I'll give to you a dress of red, stitched all around with golden thread, if you will marry me, etc.
(She)   I'll not accept your dress of red, stitched all around with golden thread, and I'll not marry you, etc.

(He) 4. I'll give to you the keys to my chest, and all the gold that I possess, if you will marry me, etc.
(She)   Yes, I'll accept the key to your chest, and all the gold that you possess, and I will marry you, etc.

PAPER OF PINS: A paper (or package) of pins doesn't sound like much of a matrimonial enticement. But when this folk song was written, pins had significant value. Even so, the object of the singer's affection was not swayed and held out until a far more substantial gift was offered.

LET ME CALL YOU SWEETHEART

Ukulele tuning: gCEA

BETH SLATER WHITSON

LEO FRIEDMAN

LET ME CALL YOU SWEETHEART: Any entertainer who has ever performed for seniors knows that this song is almost always the first and most often requested. The writing team of Friedman and Whitson also collaborated on "Meet Me Tonight In Dreamland." Both songs were million copy sellers of sheet music in the early 1900s.

More Great Guitar Books from Centerstream...

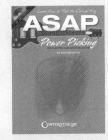

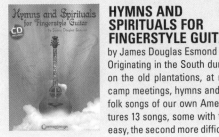

Those using
Centerstream
Books & DVDs

The Competition